Speaking of Peace

Quotations to Inspire Action

Speaking of Peace

Quotations to Inspire Action

Edited by David Krieger

Cover Art:
Pablo Picasso, *Colombe du Festival de la Jeunesse*, 1957
© 2011 Estate of Pablo Picasso / Artists Rights Society (ARS),
New York

ISBN: 1461052076
ISBN-13: 9781461052074

CONTENTS

ACKNOWLEDGMENTS

With appreciation to all the men and women whose wise words are included in this volume.

With gratitude to Carol Warner for her careful checking of the quotations for accuracy and for proofreading the manuscript.

Finally, my appreciation to the Board, staff and members of the Nuclear Age Peace Foundation who daily speak peace in words and action.

AN INVITATION

If you would like to share a quotation that you think should be included in a next edition of this volume, please send it with a citation to me at <u>dkrieger@napf.org.</u>

INTRODUCTION

When it comes to decisions on peace and war, wisdom matters. But often, such decisions, affecting the lives of millions of people, are made in haste and anger, in the midst of confusion and turmoil, without proper information or understanding. Those who make decisions about war and peace are often insulated from the results of their decisions. They are generally not the ones to suffer and die, nor are their children. In today's warfare, the burden is borne disproportionately by women and children, by those who stay home, by civilians more than combatants. Even the combatants are drawn most heavily from the poorer elements of society—young men and women responding to economic incentives, including promises of a college education.

Warfare has been largely stripped of gallantry, as powerful weapons of mass destruction, fired from afar or dropped from high altitude, have replaced soldier facing soldier. In the aftermath of the bombings of Hiroshima and Nagasaki, President Truman's Chief of Staff, Admiral William D. Leahy, lamented, "I was not taught to make war in that fashion, and wars cannot be won by destroying women and children." But that is exactly what wars do—they terrorize the innocent and foreclose the future, often leaving those who survive with both exterior and interior scars and traumas.

Initiating a war of aggression has been called the "supreme crime," for it gives rise to all the other crimes and atrocities of war, and yet those who commit this supreme crime are rarely held to account for their acts. Warfare is conducted through a series of insulating shields. Those who make decisions on war are insulated from accountability. Those who drop the bombs, fire the artillery shells and send the missiles flying generally see their targets only as blips on a radar screen. Modern warfare is mostly a long-distance affair, a cowardly means of distributing death to those who have been dehumanized as "the enemy."

Countries that initiate war are seldom spared its ravages. While leaders often walk away unscathed, such is not the case with ordinary people. It is the common man and woman and child who pay the price of war. So, it is in the interest of each of us to be skeptical in giving assent to war or becoming swept up in the frenzy of war.

War is never simple or easy. It cannot occur without a heavy price paid in life, limb and lost opportunities. Military forces that are created for defense are too easily turned to offense. In sane societies, there are many obstacles to war. War should not be left to the decision of one leader. It must be a common decision.

But where is the commitment to creating and maintaining these obstacles to war? Where is the wisdom and courage to say "No" to war? Where is the wisdom not to follow the flag, not to succumb to patriotic rhetoric by those who would send someone else's children to their deaths?

Over the years that I have worked for peace, I have found some extraordinary expressions of wisdom about peace and war from many individuals, some who lived great lives of peace and some who learned from war that it is not the answer. I have gathered the quotations in this book because it seems evident to me that humankind has reached a point in history when we badly need the accumulated wisdom of the past if we are to have a more just and peaceful future.

This book is divided into ten sections. Each has wisdom that can contribute to the possibility of creating and maintaining peace. Let me summarize the lessons of each section of this volume.

Lessons of History: If we fail to learn from the past, we are destined to repeat its mistakes.

War: War has no winners.

Peace: Peace is an imperative of the Nuclear Age, and cannot be achieved by war.

Nuclear Weapons / Nuclear War: Nuclear weapons and nuclear warfare place the future of all life at risk of annihilation.

Earth Citizenship: We are all citizens of our unique and fragile planet, the only place we know of in the universe where life exists.

Human Spirit: The human spirit has the capacity to overcome great obstacles on the path to a peaceful planet.

Commitment to Life: A commitment to protect all life is essential now and in the future.

Individual Power: Each of us can contribute to a better world and, in our own unique way, be as powerful as any human who ever walked the Earth.

Individual Responsibility: We each have a responsibility to stand for peace and human dignity.

Hope: Hope is the antidote to apathy, ignorance, complacency and despair and gives rise to action, as action gives rise to hope.

There is no goal more essential today than peace. On the wings of peace fly the hopes for humanity's future. Each of us has a role to play. We can choose peace or we can choose war. Peace will require action, while war may be the result of our inaction.

War does not happen in a vacuum. It is highly organized and requires societal support. To stop war, individuals must be willing to stand up to the war machine and those who profit from it. They must have the strength and courage to stand against the tide. In this book, you will find succinct and sometimes profoundly moving insights by many exceptional men and women, insights that can help guide us on the path to peace. I hope that you will be inspired by what you read to make a greater personal commitment to creating a more decent and peaceful world.

LESSONS OF HISTORY

The shaft of the arrow had been feathered with one of the eagle's own plumes. We often give our enemies the means of our own destruction.

~ **Aesop** (620-560 BCE), Greek fabulist

History, despite its wrenching pain, cannot be unlived, but if faced with courage doesn't need to be lived again.

~ **Maya Angelou** (b. 1928), American poet

All great historical ideas started as a utopian dream and ended with reality. Whether a particular idea remains as a utopian dream or becomes a reality depends on the number of people who believe in the ideal and their ability to act upon it.

~ **Count Richard von Coudenhove-Kalergi** (1894-1972), Austrian politician and philosopher

Power concedes nothing without a demand; it never has and it never will.

~ **Frederick Douglass** (1817-1895), American slavery abolitionist

2

Neither a wise man nor a brave man lies down on the tracks of history to wait for the train of the future to run over him.

~ **Dwight D. Eisenhower** (1890-1969), 34th U.S. President

A generation which ignores history has no past and no future.

~ **Robert Heinlein** (1907-1988), American science fiction author

Memory is where the past and the future meet. Respectfully learning the lessons of the past, we want to impress the misery of war and atomic bombing on the generations of younger people who will be tomorrow's leaders.

~ **Takashi Hiraoka** (b. 1927), former Mayor of Hiroshima, Japan

We must learn the lessons of history, that we may learn to identify and avoid the paths that lead to war.

~ **Hiroshima Peace Memorial Museum**

Memories of war must not grow dim, rather, they ought to become a stern lesson for our generation and for generations yet to come.

~ **Pope John Paul II** (1920-2005)

To remember the past is to commit oneself to the future.

~ **Pope John Paul II** (1920-2005)

The great enemy of truth is very often not the lie—deliberate, contrived, and dishonest—but the myth—persistent, persuasive, and unrealistic.

~ **John F. Kennedy** (1917-1963), 35th U.S. President

History will have to record that the greatest tragedy of this period of social transition was not the strident clamor of the bad people, but the appalling silence of the good people.

~ **Martin Luther King, Jr.** (1929-1968), American civil rights leader and 1964 Nobel Peace Laureate

Remember always...people are more important than countries.

~ **Mairead Corrigan Maguire** (b. 1944), Irish
peace activist and 1976 Nobel Peace Laureate

He who controls the past controls the future. He who controls
the present controls the past.

~ **George Orwell** (1903-1950), British author
and 1985 Nobel Laureate in Literature

Poetry comes nearer to vital truth than history.

~ **Plato** (428–348 BCE), ancient Greek philosopher

When will our consciences grow so tender that we will act to
prevent human misery rather than avenge it?

~ **Eleanor Roosevelt** (1884-1962), human rights
activist and U.S. First Lady

Those who cannot remember the past are condemned to repeat it.

~ **George Santayana** (1863-1952), British philosopher

Human history becomes more and more a race between education and catastrophe.

~ **H. G. Wells** (1866-1946), British author

WAR

Blood cannot be washed out with blood.

~ **Afghan Proverb**

Violence is the last refuge of the incompetent.

~ **Isaac Asimov** (1920-1992), American author

Every dollar spent on weapons is one less spent on schools, life-saving medicine or research into life-affirming technologies.

~ **Ban Ki-moon** (b. 1944), South Korean
diplomat and 8th United Nations Secretary-General

War: a wretched debasement of all the pretenses of civilization.

~ **General Omar N. Bradley** (1883-1981),
American military leader

There are no warlike people, just warlike leaders.

~ **Ralph Bunche** (1903-1971), American
diplomat and 1950 Nobel Peace Laureate

May the fearful consequences for winners, losers, and harmless spectators be a lesson to us all: that war is no longer, if it ever was, a viable option for humanity. If we don't learn this time, the teacher may dismiss the class in perpetuity.

~ **Adam Curle** (1916-2006), British peace educator

They have always taught and trained you to believe it to be your patriotic duty to go to war and to have yourselves slaughtered at their command. But in all the history of the world you, the people, have never had a voice in declaring war, and strange as it certainly appears, no war by any nation in any age has ever been declared by the people.

~ **Eugene V. Debs** (1855-1926), American politician

And those who have an interest in keeping the machinery of war going are a very powerful body; they will stop at nothing to make public opinion subservient to their murderous ends.

~ **Albert Einstein** (1879-1955), American physicist and 1921 Nobel Laureate in Physics

...e who joyfully marches to music in rank and file has already earned my contempt. He has been given a large brain by mistake, since for him the spinal cord would surely suffice. This disgrace to civilization should be done away with at once. Heroism at command, senseless brutality, deplorable love-of-country stance, how violently I hate all this, how despicable and ignoble war is; I would rather be torn to shreds than be part of so base an action! It is my conviction that killing under the cloak of war is nothing but an act of murder.

~ **Albert Einstein** (1879-1955), American physicist and 1921 Nobel Laureate in Physics

Every gun that is made, every warship launched, every rocket fired signifies in the final sense, a theft from those who hunger and are not fed, those who are cold and are not clothed. This world in arms is not spending money alone. It is spending the sweat of its laborers, the genius of its scientists, the hopes of its children. This is not a way of life at all in any true sense. Under the clouds of war, it is humanity hanging on a cross of iron.

~ **Dwight D. Eisenhower** (1890-1969), 34th U.S. President

After my experience, I have come to hate war. War settles nothing.

~ **Dwight D. Eisenhower** (1890-1969), 34th U.S. President

When a whole nation is roaring Patriotism at the top of its voice, I am fain to explore the cleanness of its hands and purity of its heart.

~ **Ralph Waldo Emerson** (1803-1882),
American poet

I simply can't imagine the world will ever be normal again for us. I do talk about "after the war," but it's as if I were talking about a castle in the air, something that can never come true.

~ **Anne Frank** (1929-1945), German Holocaust victim

War remains the decisive human failure.

~ **John Kenneth Galbraith** (1908-2006),
American economist

I know that war is wrong, is an unmitigated evil. I know too that it has got to go. I firmly believe that freedom won through bloodshed or fraud is no freedom.

~ **Mohandas K. Gandhi** (1869-1948), Indian independence leader

It is easier to lead men to combat, stirring up their passion, than to restrain them and direct them toward the patient labors of peace.

~ **André Gide** (1869-1951), French author and 1947 Nobel Laureate in Literature

Of course the people don't want war.... That is understood. But after all, it is the leaders of the country who determine policy, and it is always a simple matter to drag the people along, whether it's a democracy, or a fascist dictatorship, or a parliament, or a communist dictatorship. Voice or no voice, the people can always be brought to the bidding of the leaders. That is easy. All you have to do is tell them you are being attacked, and denounce the pacifists for lack of patriotism and exposing the country to danger. It works the same in any country.

~ **Hermann Goering** (1893-1946), Nazi leader

After World War II, in 1947, the U.S. Department of War, an institution of American government since 1789, was abolished and subsequently reconstituted as the Department of Defense; the Secretary of War was renamed the Secretary of Defense. And from that day to the present, the United States of America was never again in danger of war. It was in danger of defense.

~ **Joseph Heller** (1923-1999), American author

Never think that war, no matter how necessary, nor how justified, is not a crime.

~ **Ernest Hemingway** (1899-1961), American author and 1954 Nobel Laureate in Literature

The greatest threat to our world and its peace comes from those who want war, who prepare for it, and who, by holding out vague promises of future peace or by instilling fear of foreign aggression, try to make us accomplices to their plans.

~ **Hermann Hesse** (1877-1962), German author and 1946 Nobel Laureate in Literature

An enemy is one whose story we have not heard.

~ **Gene Knudsen Hoffman** (1919-2010), American peace activist

Peace is the virtue of civilization. War is its crime.

~ **Victor Hugo** (1802-1885), French author and humanitarian

War is a defeat for humanity.

~ **Pope John Paul II** (1920-2005)

Strike against war. For without you no battles can be fought! Strike against manufacturing shrapnel and gas bombs and all other tools of murder! Strike against preparedness that means death and misery to millions of human beings! Be not dumb, obedient slaves in an army of destruction! Be heroes in any army of construction!

~ **Helen Keller** (1880-1968), American author, educator and activist who was blind and deaf

War will exist until that distant day when the conscientious objector enjoys the same reputation and prestige that the warrior does today.

~ **John F. Kennedy** (1917-1963), 35th U.S. President

The ultimate weakness of violence is that it is a descending spiral, begetting the very thing it seeks to destroy. Instead of diminishing evil, it multiplies it.

~ **Martin Luther King, Jr.** (1929-1968), American civil rights leader and 1964 Nobel Peace Laureate

Our scientific power has outrun our spiritual power. We have guided missiles and misguided men.

~ **Martin Luther King, Jr.** (1929-1968), American civil rights leader and 1964 Nobel Peace Laureate

If you rejoice in victory, then you delight in killing. If you delight in killing, then you cannot fulfill yourself.

~ **Lao Tzu** (570-490 BCE), Chinese founder of Taoism

In war, as it is waged now, with the enormous losses on both sides, both sides will lose. It is a form of mutual suicide.

~ **General Douglas MacArthur** (1880-1964), American military leader

The great question is: Can global war now be outlawed from the world? If so, it would mark the greatest advance in civilization since the Sermon on the Mount. It would lift at one stroke the darkest shadow which has engulfed mankind from the beginning. It would not only remove fear and bring security—it would not only create new moral and spiritual values—it would produce an economic wave of prosperity that would raise the world's standard of living beyond anything ever dreamed of by man.

~ **General Douglas MacArthur** (1880-1964),
American military leader

War is only a cowardly escape from the problems of peace.

~ **Thomas Mann** (1875-1955), German author
and 1929 Nobel Laureate in Literature

War is wretched beyond description, and only a fool or a fraud could sentimentalize its cruel reality.

~ **John McCain** (b. 1936), American politician

If men do not now succeed in abolishing war, civilization and mankind are doomed.

~ **Ludwig von Mises** (1881-1973), Austrian political scientist

The world waits for a great nation that has the common sense, the imagination, and the faith to devote to the science and practice of nonviolence so much as a tenth of the money, brains, skill and devotion which it now devotes to the madness of war preparation. What is that nation waiting for before it undertakes its mission?

~ **A. J. Muste** (1885-1967), American peace activist

War kills and maims people. It is immoral to kill and maim people. War is immoral.

~ **Linus Pauling** (1901-1994), American academic, 1954 Nobel Laureate in Chemistry and 1962 Nobel Peace Laureate

Peace with a club in hand is war.

~ **Portuguese Proverb**

You can no more win a war than you can win an earthquake.

~ **Jeanette Rankin** (1880-1973), American
politician and pacifist

Here then, is the problem which we present to you, stark and
dreadful and inescapable: Shall we put an end to the human race; or
shall mankind renounce war?

~ **The Russell-Einstein Manifesto, 1955**

The awareness that we are all human beings together has become lost in war and through politics.

~ **Albert Schweitzer** (1875-1965), Alsatian
physician and 1952 Nobel Peace Laureate

Blood and destruction shall be so in use,
And dreadful objects so familiar
That mothers shall but smile when they behold
Their infants quartered with the hands of war.

~ **William Shakespeare** (1564-1616), British
playwright and poet

It is only those who have neither fired a shot nor heard the shrieks and groans of the wounded who cry aloud for blood, more vengeance, more desolation. War is hell.

~ **General William Tecumseh Sherman** (1820-1891), American military leader

All warfare is based on deception.

~ **Sun Tzu** (544-496 BCE), Chinese military commander

If a thousand people were not to pay their tax bills this year, that would not be a violent and bloody measure, as it would be to pay them and enable the State to commit violence and shed innocent blood.

~ **Henry David Thoreau** (1817-1862), American peace activist

The real atrocity of war is war itself, and it is an atrocity peculiar to mankind.

~ **Arnold Toynbee** (1889-1975), British historian

Wars can be waged only by human communities whose members have been conditioned and dragooned into committing this unnatural crime.

~ **Arnold Toynbee** (1889-1975), British historian

When you can make people believe absurdities, you can make them commit atrocities.

~ **Voltaire** (1694-1778), French Enlightenment philosopher

The revulsion against war not too long hence will be an almost insuperable obstacle for us to overcome. For that reason, I am convinced that we must begin now to set the machinery in motion for a permanent war economy.

~ **Charles E. Wilson** (1886-1972), American businessman, President of General Electric Company

There is no flag large enough to cover the shame of killing innocent people.

~ **Howard Zinn** (1922-2010), American historian and peace activist

PEACE

Peace is the marriage of the people and the planet, with all attendant vows.

~ Anonymous

It will be a great day when our schools get all the money they need and the Air Force has to hold a bake sale to buy a bomber.

~ Anonymous

The world is over-armed and peace is underfunded.

~ **Ban Ki-moon** (b. 1944), South Korean
diplomat and 8th United Nations Secretary-General

We simply must convert to a project of peace, laying down arms of all kinds and committing all together to building a world more worthy of man.

~ **Pope Benedict XVI** (b. 1927)

The first peace, which is the most important, is that which comes within the souls of people when they realize their relationship, their oneness with the universe and all its powers, and when they realize that at the center of the universe dwells the Great Spirit, and that this center is really everywhere, it is within each of us.

~ **Black Elk** (1863-1950), holy man of the Sioux Nation

There is no time left for anything but to make peacework a dimension of our every waking activity.

~ **Elise Boulding** (1920-2010), American sociologist and peace activist

Better than a thousand hollow words is one word that brings peace.

~ **Buddha** (560-483 BCE)

Peace, to have meaning for many who have only known suffering in both peace and war, must be translated into bread or rice, shelter, health and education, as well as freedom and human dignity.

~ **Ralph Bunche** (1904-1971), American diplomat and 1950 Nobel Peace Laureate

Peace is the only battle worth waging.

~ **Albert Camus** (1913-1960), French author and 1957 Nobel Laureate in Literature

It is far easier to make war than peace.

~ **George Clemenceau** (1841-1929), French Prime Minister

We know how to organize warfare, but do we know how to act when confronted with peace?

~ **Jacques-Yves Cousteau** (1910-1997), French ocean explorer and filmmaker

Peace can only last where human rights are respected, where the people are fed, and where individuals and nations are free.

~ **His Holiness the XIVth Dalai Lama** (b. 1935), Tibetan spiritual leader and 1989 Nobel Peace Laureate

If you want to make peace, you don't talk to your friends. You talk to your enemies.

~ **General Moshe Dyan** (1915-1981), Israeli military leader

✤ ✤ ✤

Peace cannot be kept by force. It can only be achieved by understanding.

~ **Albert Einstein** (1879-1955), American physicist and 1921 Nobel Laureate in Physics

✤ ✤ ✤

I like to believe that people in the long run are going to do more to promote peace than our governments. Indeed, I think that people want peace so much that one of these days governments had better get out of the way and let them have it.

~ **Dwight D. Eisenhower** (1890-1969), 34th U.S. President

✤ ✤ ✤

The most disadvantageous peace is better than the most just war.

~ **Desiderius Erasmus** (1469-1536), Dutch scholar

There was never a good war or a bad peace.

~ **Benjamin Franklin** (1706-1790), American
Founding Father

It is possible to live in peace.

~ **Mohandas K. Gandhi** (1869-1948), Indian
independence leader

You are not going to get peace with millions of armed men.
The chariot of peace cannot advance over a road littered with
cannons.

~ **David Lloyd George** (1863-1945), British
statesman and Prime Minister

Peace is every step.

~ **Thich Nhat Hanh** (b. 1926), Vietnamese
Buddhist philosopher

If we are peaceful, if we are happy, we can smile and blossom like a flower, and everyone in our family, our entire society, will benefit from our peace.

~ **Thich Nhat Hanh** (b. 1926), Vietnamese Buddhist philosopher

The goal toward which all history tends is peace, not peace through the medium of war, not peace through a process of universal intimidation, not peace through a program of mutual impoverishment, not peace by any means that leaves the world too weak or too frightened to go on fighting, but peace pure and simple based on that will to peace which has animated the overwhelming majority of mankind through countless ages.

~ **Robert Maynard Hutchins** (1899-1977), American educator

Nothing is more precious than peace.... Peace is the most basic starting point for the advancement of humankind.

~ **Daisaku Ikeda** (b. 1928), Japanese Buddhist philosopher

Peace will be realized only by forging bonds of trust between people at the deepest level, in the depths of their very lives.

~ **Daisaku Ikeda** (b. 1928), Japanese Buddhist philosopher

And He shall judge among the nations, and shall rebuke many people: and they shall beat their swords into ploughshares, and their spears into pruning hooks; nation shall not lift up sword against nation, neither shall they learn war any more.

~ **Isaiah 2:4**

The true and solid peace of nations consists not in equality of arms, but in mutual trust alone.

~ **Pope John XXIII** (1881-1963)

To reach peace, teach peace.

~ **Pope John Paul II** (1920-2005)

El respeto al derecho ajeno es la paz.
Peace is the respect for the rights of others.
(inscribed as a motto on the state flag of Oaxaca)

Benito Juarez (1806-1872), Mexican President

The best preparedness is the one that disarms the hostility of other nations and makes friends of them.

~ **Helen Keller** (1880-1968), American author,
educator and activist who was blind and deaf

Peace is a daily, a weekly, a monthly process, gradually changing opinions, slowly eroding old barriers, quietly building new structures. And however undramatic the pursuit of peace, the pursuit must go on.

~ **John F. Kennedy** (1917-1963), 35th U.S.
President

Peace does not rest in the charters and covenants alone. It lies in the hearts and minds of all people. So let us not rest all our hopes on parchment and on paper, let us strive to build peace, a desire for peace, a willingness to work for peace in the hearts and minds of all of our people. I believe that we can. I believe the problems of human destiny are not beyond the reach of human beings.

~ **John F. Kennedy** (1917-1963), 35th U.S. President

We will not build a peaceful world by following a negative path. It is not enough to say we must not wage war. It is necessary to love peace and sacrifice for it. We must concentrate not merely on the negative expulsion of war but on the positive affirmation of peace. We must see that peace represents a sweeter music, a cosmic melody, that is far superior to the discords of war. Somehow, we must transform the dynamics of the world power struggle from the negative nuclear arms race, which no one can win, to a positive contest to harness humanity's creative genius for the purpose of making peace and prosperity a reality for all the nations of the world.

~ **Martin Luther King, Jr.** (1929-1969), American civil rights leader and 1964 Nobel Peace Laureate

One day we must come to see that peace is not merely a distant goal that we seek, but that it is a means by which we arrive at that goal. We must pursue peaceful ends through peaceful means.

~ **Martin Luther King, Jr.** (1929-1969), American civil rights leader and 1964 Nobel Peace Laureate

If there is to be peace in the world,
There must be peace in the nations.
If there is to be peace in the nations,
There must be peace in the cities.
If there is to be peace in the cities,
There must be peace between neighbors.
If there is to be peace between neighbors,
There must be peace in the home.
If there is to be peace in the home,
There must be peace in the heart.

~ **Lao Tzu** (570-490 BCE), Chinese founder of Taoism

All we are saying is give peace a chance.

~ **John Lennon** (1940-1980), British singer and songwriter

If everyone demanded peace instead of another television set, then there'd be peace.

~ **John Lennon** (1940-1980), British singer and songwriter

As things are now going the peace we make, what peace we seem to be making, will be a peace of oil, a peace of gold, a peace of shipping, a peace...without moral purpose or human interest.

~ **Archibald MacLeish** (1907-1982), American poet

You can't separate peace from freedom because no one can be at peace unless he has his freedom.

~ **Malcolm X** (1925-1965), American civil rights leader

Blessed are the peacemakers for they shall be called the children of God.

~ **Matthew 5:9**

Winning peace means the triumph of our pledge to establish, on a democratic basis, a new social framework of tolerance and generosity from which no one will feel excluded.

~ **Federico Mayor** (b. 1934), Spanish politician and former UNESCO Director-General

Peace may sound simple—one beautiful world—but it requires everything we have, every quality, every strength, every dream, every high ideal.

~ **Yehudi Menuhin** (1916-1999), British violinist and conductor

Establishing lasting peace is the work of education; all politics can do is keep us out of war.

~ **Maria Montessori** (1870-1952), Italian educator

Dream always of a peaceful, warless, disarmed world.

~ **Robert Muller** (1923-2010), Alsatian visionary and United Nations Assistant Secretary-General

There is no way to peace; peace is the way.

~ **A. J. Muste** (1885-1967), American peace activist

Poetry is an act of peace. Peace goes into the making of a poet as flour goes into the making of bread.

~ **Pablo Neruda** (1904-1973), Chilean poet and 1971 Nobel Laureate in Literature

The more we sweat in peace the less we bleed in war.

~ **Vijaya Lakshami Pandit** (1900-1990), Indian actress and singer

If you want peace, work for justice.

~ **Pope Paul VI** (1897-1978)

This is the way of peace: overcome evil with good, falsehood with truth, and hatred with love.

~ **Peace Pilgrim** (1908-1981), American peace activist

Five enemies of peace inhabit us—avarice, ambition, envy, anger, and pride; if these were to be banished, we should infallibly enjoy perpetual peace.

~ **Petrarch** (1304-1374), Italian poet and humanist

Peace is not the product of terror or fear. Peace is not the silence of cemeteries. Peace is not the silent result of violent repression. Peace is the generous, tranquil contribution of all to the good of all. Peace is dynamism. Peace is generosity. It is right and it is duty.

~ **Archbishop Oscar Romero** (1917-1980), Salvadoran human rights activist

It isn't enough to talk about peace. One must believe in it. And it isn't enough to believe in it. One must work at it.

~ **Eleanor Roosevelt** (1884-1962), human rights activist and U.S. First Lady

The structure of world peace cannot be the work of one man or one party or one nation. It must be a peace which rests on the cooperative effort of the whole world.

~ **Franklin Delano Roosevelt** (1882-1945), 32nd U.S. President

In the hearts of people today there is a deep longing for peace. When the true spirit of peace is thoroughly dominant, it becomes an inner experience with unlimited possibilities. Only when this really happens—when the spirit of peace awakens and takes possession of men's hearts—can humanity be saved from perishing.

~ **Albert Schweitzer** (1875-1965), Alsatian physician and 1952 Nobel Peace Laureate

Peace is not an absence of war, it is a virtue, a state of mind, a disposition for benevolence, confidence, justice.

~ **Baruch Spinoza** (1632-1677), Portuguese social philosopher

Peace is the one condition of survival in this nuclear age.

~ **Adlai Stevenson** (1900-1965), American politician and diplomat

All works of love are works of peace.

~ **Mother Teresa** (1910-1997), Yugoslav humanitarian and 1979 Nobel Peace Laureate

If we have no peace, it is because we have forgotten that we belong to each other.

~ **Mother Teresa** (1910-1997), Yugoslav humanitarian and 1979 Nobel Peace Laureate

Since wars begin in the minds of men, it is in the minds of men that the defenses of peace must be constructed.

~ **UNESCO Constitution**

Aware that in the nuclear age the establishment of a lasting peace on Earth represents the primary condition for the preservation of human civilization and the survival of humankind, recognizing that the maintenance of a peaceful life for peoples is the sacred duty of each State...solemnly proclaims that the peoples of our planet have a sacred right to peace....

~ **United Nations General Assembly**
Resolution 39/11, Right of Peoples to Peace

Peace is always beautiful.

~ **Walt Whitman** (1819-1892), American poet

Peace hath higher tests of manhood than battle ever knew.

~ **John Greenleaf Whittier** (1807-1892),
American poet and slavery abolitionist

Why is war such an easy option? Why does peace remain such an elusive goal? We know statesmen skilled at waging war, but where are those dedicated enough to humanity to find a way to avoid war?

~ **Elie Wiesel** (b. 1928), American author,
educator and 1986 Nobel Peace Laureate

NUCLEAR WEAPONS /
NUCLEAR WAR

Nuclear war would obliterate all government, all culture, and possibly all human life on Earth. The endless chatter on the economy, the promise of jobs, welfare continuance, defense, justice and other aspects of our existence—including concern for the environment—is meaningless in the face of universal catastrophe.

~ **Ansel Adams** (1902-1984), American photographer

The Earth is much too small a place to accommodate both plutonium and life.

~ **Hannes Alfvén** (1908-1995), Swedish astrophysicist and 1970 Nobel Laureate in Physics

An alert and knowledgeable public can contribute greatly to convincing world leaders that a much better and safer world can be achieved by doing away with all weapons of mass destruction.

~ **Kofi Annan** (b. 1938), Ghanaian diplomat, 7th United Nations Secretary-General and 2001 Nobel Peace Laureate

We must teach an elemental truth: that status and prestige belong not to those who possess nuclear weapons, but to those who reject them.

> ~ **Ban Ki-moon** (b. 1944), South Korean
> diplomat and 8th United Nations Secretary-General

Planning nuclear war is not really a "policy" though we use the word as if blowing up the world were a defensible option instead of a crime.

> ~ **Richard J. Barnet** (1929-2004), American
> scholar and activist

We are here to make a choice between the quick and the dead. That is our business. Behind the black portent of the new atomic age lies a hope which, seized upon with faith, can work out a salvation. If we fail, then we have damned every man to be the slave of fear. Let us not deceive ourselves: we must elect world peace or world destruction.

> ~ **Bernard Baruch** (1870-1965), American
> financier and statesman

One can only encourage the efforts of the international community to ensure progressive disarmament and a world free of nuclear weapons, whose presence alone threatens the life of the planet and the ongoing integral development of the present generation and of generations yet to come.

~ **Pope Benedict XVI** (b. 1927)

I die with the conviction…that nuclear weapons are the scourge of the earth; to mine for them, manufacture them, deploy them, use them, is a curse against God, the human family, and the Earth itself.

~ **Philip Berrigan** (1923-2002), American peace activist

Nuclear weapons are incompatible with the Gospel of Jesus Christ.

~ **Robert McAfee Brown** (1920-2001),
American theologian

Nuclear weapons give no quarter. Their effects transcend time and place, poisoning the Earth and deforming its inhabitants for generation upon generation. They leave us wholly without defense, expunge all hope for survival. They hold in their sway not just the fate of nations but of civilization.

~ **General George Lee Butler** (b. 1939),
American military leader

Our technical civilization has just reached its greatest level of savagery. We will have to choose, in the more or less near future, between collective suicide and the intelligent use of our scientific conquests.

~ **Albert Camus** (1913-1960), French author and 1957 Nobel Laureate for Literature

In an all-out nuclear war, more destructive power than in all of World War II would be unleashed every second during the long afternoon it would take for all the missiles and bombs to fall. A World War II every second—more people killed in the first few hours than all the wars of history put together. The survivors, if any, would live in despair amid the poisoned ruins of a civilization that had committed suicide.

~ **Jimmy Carter** (b. 1924), 39th U.S. President

The Stone Age may return on the gleaming wings of science.

~ **Winston Churchill** (1874-1965), British Prime Minister and 1953 Nobel Laureate in Literature

Nuclear conflict is a declaration of war on the conditions that sustain human life.

~ **Norman Cousins** (1915-1990), American author and peace activist

The nuclear bomb is an equal opportunity destroyer.

~ **Ron Dellums** (b. 1935), American politician

The unleashed power of the atom has changed everything save our modes of thinking, and thus we drift toward unparalleled catastrophe.

~ **Albert Einstein** (1879-1955), American physicist and 1921 Nobel Laureate in Physics

If [the H-bomb] is successful, radioactive poisoning of the atmosphere and hence annihilation of any life on earth has been brought within the range of technical possibilities.

~ **Albert Einstein** (1879-1955), American physicist and 1921 Nobel Laureate in Physics

The world simply must not go on living in the fear of the terrible consequences of nuclear war.

~ **Dwight D. Eisenhower** (1890-1969), 34th U.S. President

What has happened to the soul of the destroying nation is yet too early to see. Forces of nature act in a mysterious manner.

> ~ **Mohandas K. Gandhi** (1869-1948), Indian independence leader

It is my firm belief that the infinite and uncontrollable fury of nuclear weapons should never be held in the hands of any mere mortal ever again, for any reason.

> ~ **Mikhail Gorbachev** (b. 1931), former President of the USSR and 1990 Nobel Peace Laureate

The nuclear danger can only be removed by abolishing nuclear weapons. But unless we address the need to demilitarize international relations, reduce military budgets, put an end to the creation of new kinds of weapons, and prevent the weaponization of outer space, all talk about a nuclear weapon-free world will be just empty rhetoric.

> ~ **Mikhail Gorbachev** (b. 1931), former President of the USSR and 1990 Nobel Peace Laureate

As scientists we understand the dangers of nuclear weapons and their devastating effects…as citizens of the world we have a duty to alert the public to the unnecessary risks that we live with every day, and to the perils we foresee if governments and societies do not take action to render nuclear weapons obsolete.

~ **Stephen Hawking** (b. 1942), British physicist

So long as such weapons exist, it is inevitable that the horror of Hiroshima and Nagasaki will be repeated.

~ **Takashi Hiraoka** (b. 1927), former Mayor of Hiroshima, Japan

For humanity to continue, we must never use nuclear weapons again. More than that, we must remove all nuclear weapons from our Earth. For that purpose, we must, hand in hand, raise our voices for the abolition of nuclear weapons. We must not annihilate the human race by fighting each other. That is the lesson of Hiroshima and Nagasaki.

~ **Takashi Hiraoka** (b. 1927), former Mayor of Hiroshima, Japan

The use of the atomic bomb, with its indiscriminate killing of women and children, revolts my soul.

~ **Herbert Hoover** (1874-1964), 31st U.S. President

The atomic bomb survivors...cannot wait another 50 years. Their highest hope is to see the abolition of nuclear weapons within their own lifetime. It is a steep climb to this goal, but one from which we must never relent.

~ **Iccho Itoh** (1945-2007), Mayor of Nagasaki, Japan

The human race cannot coexist with nuclear weapons.

~ **Iccho Itoh** (1945-2007), Mayor of Nagasaki, Japan

With the persistence of tensions and conflicts in various parts of the world, the international community must never forget what happened at Hiroshima and Nagasaki, as a warning and an incentive to develop truly effective and peaceful means of settling tensions and disputes. Fifty years after the Second World War, the leaders of nations cannot become complacent but rather should renew their commitment to disarmament and to the banishment of all nuclear weapons.

~ **Pope John Paul II** (1920-2005)

To my mind, the nuclear bomb is the most useless weapon ever invented. It can be employed to no rational purpose. It is not even an effective defense against itself. It is only something with which, in a moment of petulance or panic, you commit such fearful acts of destruction as no sane person would ever wish to have upon his conscience.

~ **George F. Kennan** (1904-2005), American diplomat

But we must remember that it has been we Americans who, at almost every step of the road, have taken the lead in the development of this sort of weaponry. It was we who first produced and tested such a device; we who were the first to raise its destructiveness to a new level with the hydrogen bomb; we who introduced the multiple warhead; we who have declined every proposal for the renunciation of the principle of "first use"; and we alone, so help us God, who have used the weapon in anger against others, and against tens of thousands of non-combatants at that.

~ **George F. Kennan** (1904-2005), American diplomat

We have gone on piling weapon upon weapon, missile upon missile, new levels of destruction upon old ones. We have done this helplessly, almost involuntarily, like victims of some sort of hypnotism, like men in a dream, like lemmings headed for the sea.

~ **George F. Kennan** (1904-2005), American diplomat

We have the power to make this the best generation of mankind in the history of the world—or to make it the last.

~ **John F. Kennedy** (1917-1963), 35th U.S. President

What in the name of God is strategic superiority? What is it politically, militarily, operationally, at these levels of [nuclear weapons] numbers? What do you do with it?

~ **Henry Kissinger** (b. 1923), former U.S.
Secretary of State and 1973 Nobel Peace Laureate

If I knew what I know now, I would never have helped to develop the bomb.

~ **George Kistiakowski** (1900-1982), chemist,
head of the Implosion Department for the
Manhattan Project

Pointing nuclear-tipped missiles at entire nations is an act of unprecedented moral depravity.

~ **Bernard Lown** (b. 1921), American
cardiologist and co-founder of 1985 Nobel Peace
Laureate organization International Physicians for
the Prevention of Nuclear War

But this very triumph of scientific annihilation—this very success of invention—has destroyed the possibility of war's ever being a medium for the practical settlement of international differences. The enormous destruction to both sides of closely matched opponents makes it impossible for even the winner to translate it into anything but his own disaster.

~ **General Douglas MacArthur** (1880-1964),
American military leader

The indefinite combination of human fallibility and nuclear weapons carries a high risk of catastrophe. Is there a military justification for continuing to accept that risk?
The answer is no.

~ **Robert S. McNamara** (1916-2009), U.S.
Secretary of Defense

To launch weapons against a nuclear-equipped opponent would be suicidal. To do so against a non-nuclear enemy would be militarily unnecessary, morally repugnant, and politically indefensible.

~ **Robert S. McNamara** (1916-2009), U.S.
Secretary of Defense

Is elimination of nuclear weapons so naïve, so simplistic, and so idealistic as to be quixotic? Some may think so. But as human beings, citizens of nations with power to influence events in the world, can we be at peace with ourselves if we strive for less? I think not.

~ **Robert S. McNamara** (1916-2009), U.S. Secretary of Defense

As a military man who has given half a century of active service, I say in all sincerity that the nuclear arms race has no military purpose. Wars cannot be fought with nuclear weapons. Their existence only adds to our perils because of the illusion which they have generated. There are powerful voices around the world who still give credence to the old Roman precept—if you desire peace, prepare for war. This is absolute nuclear nonsense and I repeat—it is a disastrous misconception to believe that by increasing the total uncertainty one increases one's own certainty.

~ **Admiral Earl Mountbatten** (1900-1979), British military leader

A new world war can hardly fail to involve the all-out use of nuclear weapons. Such a war would not drag on for years. It could all be over in a matter of days. And when it is all over what will the world be like? Our fine great buildings, our homes will exist no more. The thousands of years it took to develop our civilization will have been in vain. Our works of art will be lost. Radio, television, newspapers will disappear. There will be no means of transport. There will be no hospitals. No help can be expected for the mutilated survivors in any town to be sent from a neighboring town—there will be no neighboring towns left, no neighbors, there will be no help, there will be no hope.

~ **Admiral Earl Mountbatten** (1900-1979), British military leader

You cannot talk like sane men around a peace table while the atomic bomb itself is ticking beneath it. Do not treat the atomic bomb as a weapon of offense; do not treat it as an instrument of the police. Treat the bomb for what it is: the visible insanity of a civilization that has ceased to worship life and obey the laws of life.

~ **Lewis Mumford** (1895-1990), American philosopher of technology and science

One nuclear weapon exploded in one city—be it New York or Moscow, Islamabad or Mumbai, Toyko or Tel Aviv, Paris or Prague—could kill hundreds of thousands of people. And no matter where it happens, there is no end to what the consequences may be—for our global safety, security, society, economy, and ultimately our survival.

~ **Barack Obama** (b. 1961), 44th U.S. President and 2009 Nobel Peace Laureate

The most terrifying monster lurking in the darkness of Hiroshima is precisely the possibility that man might become no longer human.

~ **Kenzaburo Oe** (b. 1935), Japanese author and 1994 Nobel Laureate in Literature

If atomic bombs are to be added as new weapons to the arsenals of a warring world, or to the arsenals of nations preparing for war, then the time will come when mankind will curse the names of Los Alamos and Hiroshima.

~ **J. Robert Oppenheimer** (1904-1967), American theoretical physicist and Scientific Director of the Manhattan Project

We may anticipate a state of affairs in which two Great Powers will each be in a position to put an end to the civilization and life of the other, though not without risking its own. We may be likened to two scorpions in a bottle, each capable of killing the other, but only at the risk of his own life.

~ **J. Robert Oppenheimer** (1904-1967),
American theoretical physicist and Scientific
Director of the Manhattan Project

Today I can declare my hope and declare it from the bottom of my heart that we will eventually see the time when that number of nuclear weapons is down to zero and the world is a much better place.

~ **General Colin Powell** (b. 1937), former U.S.
Secretary of State

Nuclear war cannot be won and must never be fought.

~ **Ronald Reagan** (1911-2004), 40th U.S.
President

Every time you produce radiation, you produce something that has a certain half-life, in some cases for billions of years. I think the human race is going to wreck itself, and it's important that we get control of this horrible force and try to eliminate it.

> ~ **Admiral Hyman Rickover** (1900-1986),
> American military leader

The only safe counter weapon to this new power is the firm decision of mankind that it shall be used for constructive purposes only. This discovery must spell the end of war. We have been paying an ever-increasing price for indulging ourselves in this uncivilized way of settling our difficulties. We can no longer indulge in the slaughter of our young men. The price will be too high and will be paid not just by young men, but by whole populations. In the past we have given lip service to the desire for peace. Now we must meet the test of really working to achieve something basically new in the world.

> ~ **Eleanor Roosevelt** (1884-1962), human rights
> activist and U.S. First Lady

That's what nuclear bombs do, whether they're used or not. They violate everything that is human; they alter the meaning of life. Why do we tolerate them? Why do we tolerate the men who use nuclear weapons to blackmail the entire human race?

> ~ **Arundhati Roy** (b. 1961), Indian novelist and
> activist

So there's an understandable tendency to think that the problem of nuclear war has been solved, or at least is being solved—that we can now ignore it and turn our attention to the formidable array of other pressing problems. This opinion is surprisingly widespread. It is, we believe, a dangerous illusion.

~ **Carl Sagan** (1934-1996), American astronomer
and planetary scientist

There is no issue more important than the avoidance of nuclear war. Whatever your interests, passions or goals, they and you are threatened fundamentally by the prospect of nuclear war. We have achieved the capability for the certain destruction of our civilization and perhaps of our species as well. I find it incredible that any thinking person would not be concerned in the deepest way about this issue.

~ **Carl Sagan** (1934-1996), American astronomer
and planetary scientist

There is no cause more urgent, no dedication more fitting for us than to strive to eliminate the threat of nuclear war. No social convention, no political system, no economic hypothesis, no religious dogma more important.

~ **Carl Sagan** (1934-1996), American astronomer
and planetary scientist

With each year that passes, nuclear weapons provide their possessors with less safety while provoking more danger. The walls dividing the nations of the two-tiered [nuclear] world are crumbling.

~ **Jonathan Schell** (b. 1943), American author

The moral cost of nuclear armament is that it makes of all of us underwriters of the slaughter of hundreds of millions of people and the cancellation of future generations.

~ **Jonathan Schell** (b. 1943), American author

We prepare for our extinction in order to ensure our survival. If our species does destroy itself, it will be a death in the cradle—a case of infant mortality.

~ **Jonathan Schell** (b. 1943) American author

Those who conduct an atomic war for freedom will die, or end their lives miserably. Instead of freedom they will find destruction. Radioactive clouds resulting from a war between East and West would imperil humanity everywhere.... An atomic war is therefore the most senseless and lunatic act that could ever take place. At all costs it must be prevented.

~ **Albert Schweitzer** (1875-1965), Alsatian
physician and 1952 Nobel Peace Laureate

The nuclear club should be abolished and anybody who has a nuclear weapon is the enemy of mankind.

~ **George Shultz** (b. 1920), former U.S. Secretary of State

The poisoning of arrowheads and of water supplies; who winces at this any longer, now that we have dropped two poisonous atomic bombs on Japan and have stockpiled enough of them to extinguish all life on this planet?

~ **Arnold Toynbee** (1889-1975), British historian

There is nothing more urgent confronting the people of all nations than the banning of all nuclear weapons under a foolproof system of international control.

~ **Harry S. Truman** (1884-1972), 33rd U.S. President

Starting an atomic war is totally unthinkable for rational men.

~ **Harry S. Truman** (1884-1972), 33rd U.S. President

Nuclear abolition is the democratic wish of the world's people, and has been our goal almost since the dawn of the atomic age. Together, we have the power to decide whether the nuclear era ends in a bang or worldwide celebration.

~ **Archbishop Desmond Tutu** (b. 1931),
South African human rights activist and 1984
Nobel Peace Laureate

Nuclear disarmament is not an option for governments to take up or ignore. It is a moral duty owed by them to their own citizens, and to humanity as a whole. We must not await another Hiroshima or Nagasaki before finally mustering the political will to banish these weapons from global arsenals.

~ **Archbishop Desmond Tutu** (b. 1931),
South African human rights activist and 1984
Nobel Peace Laureate

We write in defense of creation. We do so because the creation itself is under attack. Air and water, trees and fruits and flowers, birds and fish and cattle, all children and youth, women and men live under the darkening shadows of a threatening nuclear winter.

~ **United Methodist Council of Bishops**

If we fail to seize the moment, history will never forgive us—if there is a history.

> ~ **Thomas J. Watson** (1874-1956), American businessman, President of International Business Machines (IBM)

Anti-nuclear civil resistance is the right of every citizen of this planet. For the nuclear threat, attacking as it does every core concept of human rights, calls for urgent and universal action for its prevention.

> ~ **Judge Christopher Weeramantry** (b. 1926), Sri Lankan jurist and former Vice-President of the International Court of Justice

I don't know how great the chance is that the world will survive the next few decades and not be plunged into a nuclear war. If any human beings are alive 50 years from now, they may look back on today's situation as a virulent case of collective mental disease that gripped humanity.

> ~ **Victor Weisskopf** (1908-2002), American theoretical physicist who worked on the Manhattan Project

EARTH CITIZENSHIP

People are afraid to move into the free fall of a totally new way of looking at others. So the new mythology to come must be a global mythology, and it's got to solve the problem of the in-group by showing there's no out-group. We're all members of a society of the planet, not of one particular place.... There must be brotherhood and cooperation. Because unless that comes, we're going to blow ourselves to smithereens.

> ~ **Joseph Campbell** (1904-1987), American mythologist

The big challenge is education—an inner education so that the person identifies himself with "humanity" rather than with the in-group. Now, that isn't easy because humanity is a vague concept, and the in-group is what you're experiencing.

> ~ **Joseph Campbell** (1904-1987), American mythologist

The love of country is a splendid thing. But why should love stop at the border?

> ~ **Pablo Casals** (1876-1973), Catalan cellist and conductor

Our generation has arrived at the threshold of a new era in human history: the birth of a global community. Modern communications, trade and international relations as well as the security and environmental dilemmas we all face make us increasingly interdependent. No one can live in isolation. Thus, whether we like it or not, our vast and diverse human family must finally learn to live together. Individually and collectively we must assume a greater sense of Universal Responsibility.

~ **His Holiness the XIVth Dalai Lama** (b. 1935),
Tibetan spiritual leader and 1989 Nobel Peace Laureate

With all my heart I believe that the world's present system of sovereign nations can lead only to barbarism, war and inhumanity. There is no salvation for civilization, or even the human race, other than the creation of a world government.

~ **Albert Einstein** (1879-1955), American
physicist and 1921 Nobel Laureate in Physics

We earn a right to exist only if we fulfill our duty as citizens of the world.

~ **Mohandas K. Gandhi** (1869-1948), Indian
independence leader

If the future of mankind is not to be jeopardized by conflicting spheres of civilization and culture, we have no alternative but to shift the ray of our attention from that which separates us to that which unites us. Mine is a vision of a United Nations consisting not—as happens so frequently today—of divided nations but of united people, belonging to a world in jeopardy which can be saved only by uniting all human forces.

~ **Vaclav Havel** (b. 1936), playwright and first President of Czech Republic

Maluna a'e o na lahui apau ke ola o ke kanaka.
Above all nations is humanity.

~ **Hawaii State Motto**

We are one human family, by simply being born into this world; we are one inheritance and one stock with every other human being. This oneness expresses itself in all the richness and diversity of the human family: in different races, cultures, languages and histories. And we are called to recognize the basic solidarity of the human family as the fundamental condition of our life together on this earth.

~ **Pope John Paul II** (1920-2005)

Join with the Earth and each other, to bring new life to the land, to restore the waters, to refresh the air, to renew the forests, to care for the plants, to protect the creatures, to celebrate the seas, to rejoice in the sunlight, to sing the song of the stars, to recall our destiny, to renew our spirits, to reinvigorate our bodies, to recreate the human community, to promote justice and peace, to love our children and love one another, to join together as many and diverse expressions of one loving mystery, for the healing of the Earth and the renewal of all life.

~ **Martin Luther King, Jr.** (1929-1968), American civil rights leader and 1964 Nobel Peace Laureate

Anyone who has been in space knows that the impatiently awaited unearthliness quickly loses its charm. It is not the boring uniform blackness of the cosmic abyss that engages your attention, but the spectacle of our small planet haloed in blue. Suddenly, you get a feeling you've never had before, that you are an inhabitant of Earth.

~ **Olig Makarov** (1968-2003), Russian cosmonaut

The Earth Flag is my symbol of the task before us all. We are the custodians of the future of the Earth. Unless we check the rapacious exploitations of our Earth and protect it, we have endangered the future of our children and our children's children. It reminds me of how helpless this planet is—something that we must hold in our arms and care for.

~ **Margaret Mead** (1901-1978), American
cultural anthropologist

This is the moment when we must come together to save this planet.

~ **Barack Obama** (b. 1961), 44th U.S. President
and 2009 Nobel Peace Laureate

My country is the world, and my religion is to do good.

~ **Thomas Paine** (1737-1809), American
revolutionary and pamphleteer

The first day we pointed to our countries. The third day, we pointed to our continents. By the fifth day, we were aware of only one Earth.

~ **Sultan bin Salman Al-Saud** (b. 1956), Saudi
astronaut

You see the Earth as a bright blue and white Christmas tree ornament in the sky. It's so small and so fragile. You realize that on that small spot is everything that means anything to you, all of history and art and death and birth and love.

> ~ **Russell Schweikart** (b. 1935), American astronaut

The Earth does not belong to man; man belongs to Earth. Man did not weave the web of life, he is merely a strand in it. Whatever he does to the web, he does to himself.

> ~ **Chief Seattle** (1786-1866), Duwamish tribal leader

I am not an Athenian or a Greek, but a citizen of the world.

> ~ **Socrates** (470–399 BCE), ancient Greek philosopher (as quoted by Plutarch)

We travel together, passengers on a little space ship, dependent on its vulnerable reserves of air and soil; all committed for our safety to its security and peace; preserved from annihilation only by the care, the work, and I will say, the love we give our fragile craft. We cannot maintain it half fortunate, half miserable, half confident, half despairing, half slave to the ancient enemies of man half free in a liberation of resources undreamed of until this day. No craft, no crew can travel with such vast contradictions. On their resolution depends the survival of us all.

> ~ **Adlai Stevenson** (1900-1965), American
> politician and diplomat

The age of nations is past. The task before us now, if we would not perish, is to shake off our ancient prejudices, and to build the Earth.

> ~ **Pierre Teilhard de Chardin** (1881-1955),
> French philosopher and Jesuit priest

HUMAN SPIRIT

Even in our sleep
Pain that we cannot forget
Falls drop by drop upon the heart
Until in our own despair
Against our will
Comes wisdom
Through the awful grace of God.

> ~ **Aeschylus** (525–456 BCE), Greek tragedian

Now, I truly believe that we in this generation must come to terms with nature, and I think we're challenged as mankind has never been challenged before to prove our maturity and our mastery, not of nature, but of ourselves.

> ~ **Rachel Carson** (1907-1964), American marine biologist and nature writer

The most important human endeavor is the striving for morality in our actions. Our inner balance and even our very existence depend on it. Only morality in our actions can give beauty and dignity to life.

> ~ **Albert Einstein** (1879-1955), American physicist and 1921 Nobel Laureate in Physics

In order to be an immaculate member of a flock of sheep, one must above all be a sheep oneself.

> ~ **Albert Einstein** (1879-1955), American
> physicist and 1921 Nobel Laureate in Physics

You have to stand against the whole world although you may have to stand alone. You have to stare at the world in the face although the world may look at you with bloodshot eyes. Do not fear. Trust that little thing that resides in your heart.

> ~ **Mohandas K. Gandhi** (1869-1948), Indian
> independence leader

As human beings, our greatness lies not so much in being able to remake the world—that is the myth of the "atomic age"—as in being able to remake ourselves.

> ~ **Mohandas K. Gandhi** (1869-1948), Indian
> independence leader

Keep your face to the sunshine and you cannot see your shadow. It's what sunflowers do.

> ~ **Helen Keller** (1880-1968), American author,
> educator and activist who was blind and deaf

Our lives begin to end the day we become silent about things that matter.

~ **Martin Luther King, Jr.** (1929-1969), American civil rights leader and 1964 Nobel Peace Laureate

Acting upon my principles became incompatible with my role in the military. By putting down my weapon, I chose to reassert myself as a human being.

~ **Camilo Mejia** (b. 1975), American anti-war activist

He who fights against monsters should see to it that he does not become a monster in the process. And when you stare persistently into an abyss, the abyss stares into you.

~ **Friedrich Nietzsche** (1844-1900), German philosopher

Change will not come if we wait for some other person or some other time. We are the ones we've been waiting for. We are the change that we seek.

~ **Barack Obama** (b. 1961), 44th U.S. President and 2009 Nobel Peace Laureate

The quest for a war-free world has a basic purpose: survival. But if in the process we learn how to achieve it by love rather than by fear, by kindness rather than by compulsion; if in the process we learn to combine the essential with the enjoyable, the expedient with the benevolent, the practical with the beautiful, this will be an extra incentive to embark on this great task. Above all, remember your humanity.

> ~ **Joseph Rotblat** (1908-2005), British physicist and 1995 Nobel Peace Laureate

We have become far too clever to survive without wisdom.

> ~ **E.F. Schumacher** (1911-1977), British economist

My humanity is bound up in yours, for we can only be human together.

> ~ **Achbishop Desmond Tutu** (b. 1931), South African human rights activist and 1984 Nobel Peace Laureate

We hold these truths to be self-evident, that all men are created equal, that they are endowed by their Creator with certain unalienable rights, that among these are Life, Liberty, and the pursuit of Happiness.

~ United States Declaration of Independence

COMMITMENT TO LIFE

The greatest tragedy is not to live and die, we all must. The greatest tragedy is for a person to live and die without the satisfaction of giving life to others.

~ **Cesar E. Chavez** (1927-1993), American labor leader and civil rights activist

Let us not forget that our children and grandchildren will be part of that society of the future and it is our duty to work as soon as today to assure them the joy of living and the pride to be human beings.

~ **Jacques-Yves Cousteau** (1910-1997), French ocean explorer and filmmaker

Dear Posterity: If you have not become more just, more peaceful, and in general more sensible than we are (or were) today, then may the Devil take you! Respectfully expressing his opinion with this devout hope is (or was) your Albert Einstein. (Placed in cornerstone of publishing house building in New York in 1936.)

~ **Albert Einstein** (1879-1955), American physicist and 1921 Nobel Laureate in Physics

There are only two ways to live your life. One is as though nothing is a miracle. The other is as if everything is.

> ~ **Albert Einstein** (1879-1955), American physicist and 1921 Nobel Laureate in Physics

Nonviolence is absolute respect for each human being.

> ~ **Adolpho Perez Esquival** (b. 1931), Argentine artist, peace activist and 1980 Nobel Peace Laureate

We are not a perfect people. Yet we are called to a perfect mission—to feed the hungry, to clothe the naked, to house the homeless, to teach the illiterate, to provide jobs for the jobless, and to choose the human race over the nuclear race.

> ~ **Reverend Jesse Jackson** (b. 1941), American civil rights leader

We must encourage all people of good will to join the work of abolishing war and weapons—not out of fear of dying, but out of the joy of living.

> ~ **Mairead Corrigan Maguire** (b. 1944), Irish peace activist and 1976 Nobel Peace Laureate

All of us share this world for but a brief moment in time. The question is whether we spend that time focused on what pushes us apart or whether we commit ourselves to an effort, a sustained effort to find common ground, to focus on the future we seek for our children and to respect the dignity of all human beings.

~ **Barack Obama** (b. 1961), 44th U.S. President and 2009 Nobel Peace Laureate

I cannot but have reverence for all that is called life. I cannot avoid compassion for everything that is called life. That is the beginning and foundation of morality.

~ **Albert Schweitzer** (1875-1965), Alsatian physician and 1952 Nobel Peace Laureate

Ethics, too, are nothing but reverence for life. This is what gives me the fundamental principle of morality, namely, that good consists in maintaining, promoting, and enhancing life, and that destroying, injuring, and limiting life are evil.

~ **Albert Schweitzer** (1875-1965), Alsatian physician and 1952 Nobel Peace Laureate

Because there is global insecurity, nations are engaged in a mad arms race, spending billions of dollars wastefully on instruments of destruction, when millions are starving. Just a fraction of what is expended obscenely on defense budgets, would make the difference in enabling God's children to fill their stomachs, be educated, and given the chance, to lead happy and fulfilled lives.

~ **Archbishop Desmond Tutu** (b. 1931), South African human rights activist and 1984 Nobel Peace Laureate

As we open the gates of our memory, as we look back at what has been, we always must remember that it is given to men and women to choose life and living, not death and destruction.

~ **Elie Wiesel** (b. 1928), American author, educator and 1986 Nobel Peace Laureate

INDIVIDUAL POWER

Hope for the Earth lies not with leaders, but in your own heart and soul. If you decide to save the Earth, it will be saved. Each person can be as powerful as the most powerful person who ever lived—and that is you, if you love this planet.

> ~ **Helen Caldicott** (b. 1938), Australian
> physician and peace activist

There is nothing more powerful than an individual acting out of conscience, thus bringing the collective conscience to life.

> ~ **Norman Cousins** (1915-1990), American
> author and educator

The time has come when speaking is not enough, applauding is not enough. We have to act. I urge you every time you have the opportunity, make your opinions known by a physical presence. Do it!

> ~ **Jacques-Yves Cousteau** (1910-1997), French
> ocean explorer and filmmaker

What lies before us and what lies behind us are small matters compared to what lies within us.

> ~ **Ralph Waldo Emerson** (1803-1882),
> American poet

Only one individual is necessary to spread the leavening influence of ahimsa [nonviolence] in an office, a business, a school, or even a large institution.

> ~ **Mohandas K. Gandhi** (1869-1948), Indian independence leader

Some believe there is nothing one man or one woman can do against the enormous array of the world's ills—against misery, against ignorance, or injustice and violence. Yet many of the world's great movements, of thought and action, have flowed from the work of a single man. A young monk began the Protestant reformation, a young general extended an empire from Macedonia to the borders of the earth, and a young woman reclaimed the territory of France. It was a young Italian explorer who discovered the New World, and 32-year-old Thomas Jefferson who proclaimed that all men are created equal. "Give me a place to stand," said Archimedes, "and I will move the world." These men moved the world, and so can we all.

> ~ **Robert F. Kennedy** (1925-1968), American politician

Each time a man stands up for an ideal, or acts to improve the lot of others, or strikes out against injustice, he sends forth a tiny ripple of hope, and crossing each other from a million different centers of energy and daring, those ripples build a current which can sweep down the mightiest walls of oppression and resistance.

~ **Robert F. Kennedy** (1925-1968), American politician

Change does not roll in on the wheels of inevitability, but comes through continuous struggle.

~ **Martin Luther King, Jr.** (1929-1968), American civil rights leader and 1964 Nobel Peace Laureate

People usually fail when they are on the verge of success. So give as much care to the end as to the beginning.

~ **Lao Tzu** (570-490 BCE), Chinese founder of Taoism

One man in the right makes a majority.

> ~ **Abraham Lincoln** (1809-1865), 16th U.S. President

Never doubt that a small group of thoughtful, committed citizens can change the world; indeed, it's the only thing that ever has.

> ~ **Margaret Mead** (1901-1978), American cultural anthropologist

For all the cruelty and hardship of our world, we are not mere prisoners of fate. Our actions matter and can bend history in the direction of justice.

> ~ **Barack Obama** (b. 1961), 44th U.S. President and 2009 Nobel Peace Laureate

It is not because things are difficult that we do not dare, it is because we do not dare that things are difficult.

> ~ **Seneca** (4 BCE-65 CE), Roman philosopher and politician

We sometimes feel that what we do is just a drop in the ocean, but the ocean would be less because of that missing drop.

~ **Mother Teresa** (1910-1997), Yugoslav humanitarian and 1979 Nobel Peace Laureate

We cannot do great things, only small things with great love.

~ **Mother Teresa** (1910-1997), Yugoslav humanitarian and 1979 Nobel Peace Laureate

I know of no more encouraging fact than the unquestionable ability of man to elevate his life by conscious endeavor.

~ **Henry David Thoreau** (1817-1862), American author and peace activist

Revolutionary change does not come as one cataclysmic moment...but as an endless succession of surprises, moving zigzag toward a more decent society. We don't have to engage in grand, heroic actions to participate in the process of change. Small acts, when multiplied by millions of people, can transform the world.

~ **Howard Zinn** (1922-2010), American historian and peace activist

INDIVIDUAL RESPONSIBILITY

Nothing could be worse than fear that one has given up too soon and left one effort unexpended which might have saved the world.

> ~ **Jane Addams** (1860-1935), American peace
> activist and 1931 Nobel Peace Laureate

There is no trust more sacred than the one the world holds with children. There is no duty more important than ensuring that their rights are respected, that their welfare is protected, that their lives are free from fear and want and that they grow up in peace.

> ~ **Kofi Annan** (b. 1938), Ghanaian diplomat,
> 7th United Nations Secretary-General and 2001
> Nobel Peace Laureate

Ours is a world of nuclear giants and ethical infants. We know more about war than we know about peace, more about killing than we know about living. We have grasped the mystery of the atom and rejected the Sermon on the Mount.

> ~ **General Omar N. Bradley** (1893-1981),
> American military leader

The only thing necessary for the triumph of evil is for good men to do nothing.

> ~ **Edmund Burke** (1729-1797), Irish political philosopher

Real generosity toward the future lies in giving all to the present.

> ~ **Albert Camus** (1913-1960), French author and 1957 Nobel Laureate in Literature

We all have a stake in the security of the 21st century, and we must all work together to eliminate the dangers posed by weapons of mass destruction as we strive to free our world from the fear of the catastrophe of war.

> ~ **Helen Clark** (b. 1950), former Prime Minister of New Zealand

It does not matter how slowly you go as long as you do not stop.

> ~ **Confucius** (551-479 BCE), Chinese social philosopher

No man is an Iland,
intire of itselfe; every man is a peece
of the Continent, a part of the maine;
if a Clod bee washed away
by the Sea, Europe is the lesse,
as well as if the Promontorie were,
as well as if a Mannor of thy friends
or of thine owne were;
any man's death diminishes me,
because I am involved in Mankinde;
And therefore never send to know
for whom the bell tolls;
It tolls for thee.

~ **John Donne** (1573-1631), British poet

I think of a hero as someone who understands the degree of responsibility that comes with his freedom.

~ **Bob Dylan** (b. 1941), American singer and songwriter

Only an alert and knowledgeable citizenry can compel the proper meshing of the huge industrial and military machinery of defense with our peaceful methods and goals, so that security and liberty may prosper together.

~ **Dwight D. Eisenhower** (1890-1969), 34th U.S. President

Consciously or unconsciously, every one of us does render some service or other. If we cultivate the habit of doing this service deliberately, our desire for service will steadily grow stronger, and will make not only for our own happiness, but that of the world at large.... All of us are bound to place our resources at the disposal of humanity.

~ **Mohandas K. Gandhi** (1869-1948), Indian independence leader

The future is challenging us. But humanity is capable of meeting the challenge. We will meet the challenge if we become aware of the world's unity, of humankind's common diversity, and of the responsibility of every one of us for the preservation of life on Earth.

~ **Mikhail Gorbachev** (b. 1931), former President of the USSR and 1990 Nobel Peace Laureate

In matters of preserving peace and saving mankind from the threat of nuclear war, let no one remain indifferent or stand aloof. This concerns all and everyone. Each state, large or small, socialist or capitalist, has an important contribution to make. Every responsible political party, every public organization and every person can also make an important contribution.

~ **Mikhail Gorbachev** (b. 1931), former President of the USSR and 1990 Nobel Peace Laureate

I am only one,
But still I am one.
I cannot do everything,
But still I can do something;
And because I cannot do everything
I will not refuse to do the something that I can do.

~ **Edward Everett Hale** (1822-1909), American
poet

The salvation of this human world lies nowhere else than in the human heart, in the human power to reflect, in human meekness, and in human responsibility.

~ **Vaclav Havel** (b. 1936), playwright and first
President of Czech Republic

Without a global revolution in the sphere of human consciousness, nothing will change for the better in the sphere of our being as humans, and the catastrophe toward which this world is headed—be it ecological, social, demographic, or a general breakdown of civilization—will be unavoidable.

~ **Vaclav Havel** (b. 1936), playwright and first
President of Czech Republic

We must never forget that the record on which we judge these defendants today is the record on which history will judge us tomorrow. To pass these defendants a poisoned chalice is to put it to our own lips as well.

> ~ **Justice Robert Jackson** (1892-1954), chief U.S. prosecutor at the Nuremberg Tribunal

If certain acts in violation of treaties are crimes they are crimes whether the United States does them or whether Germany does them, and we are not prepared to lay down a rule of criminal conduct against others which we would not be willing to have invoked against us.

> ~ **Justice Robert Jackson** (1892-1954), chief U.S. prosecutor at the Nuremberg Tribunal

If humanity is to have a hopeful future, there is no escape from the pre-eminent involvement and responsibility of the single human soul, in all its loneliness and frailty.

> ~ **George F. Kennan** (1904-2005), American diplomat

First they came for the Jews and I did not speak out—because I was not a Jew. Then they came for the communists and I did not speak out—because I was not a communist. Then they came for the trade unionists and I did not speak out—because I was not a trade unionist. Then they came for me—and there was no one left to speak out for me.

~ **Martin Niemöller** (1892-1984), German pastor and social activist

Responsibility is a unique concept. It can only reside and adhere in a single individual. You may share it with others, but your portion is not diminished. You may disclaim it, but you cannot divest yourself of it. If responsibility is rightfully yours, no evasion or ignorance or passing the blame can shift the burden on someone else.

~ **Admiral Hyman Rickover** (1900-1986), U.S. military leader

We are rare and precious because we are alive, because we can think. We are privileged to live, to influence and control our future. I believe we have an obligation to fight for that life, to struggle not just for ourselves, but for all those creatures who came before us, and to whom we are beholden, and for all those who, if we are wise enough, will come after us.

~ **Carl Sagan** (1934-1996), American astronomer and planetary scientist

If we do not speak for Earth, who will? If we are not committed to our own survival, who will be?

~ **Carl Sagan** (1934-1996), American astronomer
and planetary scientist

All it takes for evil to rule a land is for good men to remain silent.

~ **Daniel Webster** (1782-1852), American politician

If I have to recapitulate in a few words what I feel is the most important commandment for our generation, it is to fight indifference. Whatever happened, happened not only because the killer killed, but because the world was indifferent.

~ **Elie Wiesel** (b. 1928), American author,
educator and 1986 Nobel Peace Laureate

As soon as you say the topic is civil disobedience, you are saying our *problem* is civil disobedience. That is *not* our problem. Our problem is civil *obedience*. Our problem is the numbers of people all over the world who have obeyed the dictates of the leaders of their government and have gone to war, and millions have been killed because of this obedience.... Our problem is that people are obedient all over the world, in the face of poverty and starvation and stupidity, and war, and cruelty. Our problem is that people are obedient while the jails are full of petty thieves, and all the while the grand thieves are running the country. That's our problem.

~ **Howard Zinn** (1922-2010), American historian and peace activist

HOPE

Hope has two beautiful daughters: their names are anger and courage. Anger that things are the way they are. Courage to make them the way they ought to be.

> ~ **Saint Augustine** (354-436), ancient Roman philosopher and theologian

What oxygen is to the lungs, such is hope to the meaning of life.

> ~ **Emil Brunner** (1889-1966), Swiss theologian

Too much sanity may be madness and the maddest of all, to see life as it is and not as it should be.

> ~ **Miguel de Cervantes** (1547-1616), Spanish author of *Don Quixote*

The capacity for hope is the most significant fact of life. It provides human beings with a sense of destination and the energy to get started.

> ~ **Norman Cousins** (1915-1990), American author and educator

"Hope" is the thing with feathers
That perches in the soul
And sings the tune without the words
And never stops—at all.

~ **Emily Dickinson** (1830-1886), American poet

In the middle of difficulty lies opportunity.

~ **Albert Einstein** (1879-1955), American
physicist and 1921 Nobel Laureate in Physics

We judge a man's wisdom by his hope.

~ **Ralph Waldo Emerson** (1803-1882),
American poet

The test of a first-rate intelligence is the ability to hold two
opposed ideas in mind at the same time and still retain the ability
to function. One should, for example, be able to see that things are
hopeless and yet be determined to make them otherwise.

~ **F. Scott Fitzgerald** (1896-1940), American author

It's really a wonder that I haven't dropped all my ideals, because they seem so absurd and impossible to carry out. Yet I keep them, because in spite of everything I still believe that people are really good at heart. I simply can't build my hopes on a foundation consisting of confusion, misery and death.

~ **Anne Frank** (1929-1945), German Holocaust victim

To hope means to be ready at every moment for that which is not yet born, and yet not become desperate if there is no birth in our lifetime.

~ **Erich Fromm** (1900-1980), American humanistic philosopher

When I despair, I remember that all through history the way of truth and love has always won. There have been tyrants and murderers and for a time they seem invincible but in the end, they always fall—think of it, always.

~ **Mohandas K. Gandhi** (1869-1948), Indian independence leader

In all things it is better to hope than to despair.

~ **Johann Wolfgang von Goethe** (1749-1832),
German philosopher

Hope is not prognostication. It is an orientation of the spirit, an orientation of the heart; it transcends the world that is immediately experienced, and is anchored somewhere beyond its horizons.

~ **Vaclav Havel** (b. 1936), playwright and first
President of Czech Republic

Hope is not the conviction that something will turn out well, but the certainty that something makes sense, regardless of how it turns out.

~ **Vaclav Havel** (b. 1936), playwright and first
President of Czech Republic

If humanity is to maintain hope for the future, we must act now with courage and decisiveness to achieve a nuclear-free world.

~ **Takashi Hiraoka** (b. 1927), former Mayor of
Hiroshima, Japan

Only when life and human rights are accorded the highest priority can young people enjoy lives of boundless hope.

> ~ **Takashi Hiraoka** (b. 1927), former Mayor of Hiroshima, Japan

Optimism is the faith that leads to achievement. Nothing can be done without hope or confidence.

> ~ **Helen Keller** (1880-1968), American author, educator and activist who was blind and deaf

We must accept finite disappointment, but never lose infinite hope.

> ~ **Martin Luther King, Jr.** (1929-1968), American civil rights leader and 1964 Nobel Peace Laureate

Everything that is done in the world is done by hope.

> ~ **Martin Luther King, Jr.** (1929-1968), American civil rights leader and 1964 Nobel Peace Laureate

Nothing that is worth doing can be achieved in our lifetime; therefore we must be saved by hope. Nothing which is true or beautiful or good makes complete sense in any immediate context of history; therefore we must be saved by faith. Nothing we do, however virtuous, can be accomplished alone; therefore we must be saved by love.

~ **Reinhold Niebuhr** (1892-1971), American Protestant theologian

Once you choose hope, anything's possible.

~ **Christopher Reeve** (1952-2004), American actor

The future belongs to those who believe in the beauty of their dreams.

~ **Eleanor Roosevelt** (1884-1962), human rights activist and U.S. First Lady

The future belongs to those who see a future.

~ **Joseph Rotblat** (1908-2005), British physicist and 1995 Nobel Peace Laureate

Not only is another world possible, she is on her way. On a quiet day, I can hear her breathing.

> ~ **Arundhati Roy** (b. 1961), Indian novelist and peace activist

The future of civilization depends on our overcoming the meaninglessness and hopelessness that characterizes the thoughts of men today.

> ~ **Albert Schweitzer** (1875-1965), Alsatian physician and 1952 Nobel Peace Laureate

Hope is believing in spite of the evidence, then watching the evidence change.

> ~ **Jim Wallis** (b. 1948), American Christian theologian and political activist

I have learned two lessons in my life: first, there are no sufficient literary, psychological, or historical answers to human tragedy, only moral ones. Second, just as despair can come to one another only from other human beings, hope, too, can be given to one only by other human beings.

> ~ **Elie Wiesel** (b. 1928), American author, educator and 1986 Nobel Peace Laureate

Appendix I
The Russell-Einstein Manifesto
Issued in London, 9 July 1955

In the tragic situation which confronts humanity, we feel that scientists should assemble in conference to appraise the perils that have arisen as a result of the development of weapons of mass destruction, and to discuss a resolution in the spirit of the appended draft.

We are speaking on this occasion, not as members of this or that nation, continent, or creed, but as human beings, members of the species Man, whose continued existence is in doubt. The world is full of conflicts; and, overshadowing all minor conflicts, the titanic struggle between Communism and anti-Communism.

Almost everybody who is politically conscious has strong feelings about one or more of these issues; but we want you, if you can, to set aside such feelings and consider yourselves only as members of a biological species which has had a remarkable history, and whose disappearance none of us can desire.

We shall try to say no single word which should appeal to one group rather than to another. All, equally, are in peril, and, if the peril is understood, there is hope that they may collectively avert it.

We have to learn to think in a new way. We have to learn to ask ourselves, not what steps can be taken to give military victory to whatever group we prefer, for there no longer are such steps; the question we have to ask ourselves is: what steps can be taken to prevent a military contest of which the issue must be disastrous to all parties?

The general public, and even many men in positions of authority, have not realized what would be involved in a war with nuclear bombs. The general public still thinks in terms of the obliteration of cities. It is understood that the new bombs are more powerful than the old, and that, while one A-bomb could obliterate Hiroshima, one H-bomb could obliterate the largest cities, such as London, New York, and Moscow.

No doubt in an H-bomb war great cities would be obliterated. But this is one of the minor disasters that would have to be faced. If everybody in London, New York, and Moscow were exterminated, the world might, in the course of a few centuries, recover from the blow. But we now know, especially since the Bikini test, that nuclear bombs can gradually spread destruction over a very much wider area than had been supposed.

It is stated on very good authority that a bomb can now be manufactured which will be 2,500 times as powerful as that which destroyed Hiroshima. Such a bomb, if exploded near the ground or under water, sends radio-active particles into the upper air. They sink gradually and reach the surface of the earth in the form of a deadly dust or rain. It was this dust which infected the Japanese fishermen and their catch of fish. No one knows how widely such lethal radio-active particles might be diffused, but the best authorities are unanimous in saying that a war with H-bombs might possibly put an end to the human race. It is feared that if many H-bombs are used there will be universal death, sudden only for a minority, but for the majority a slow torture of disease and disintegration.

Many warnings have been uttered by eminent men of science and by authorities in military strategy. None of them will say that the worst results are certain. What they do say is that these results are possible, and no one can be sure that they will not be realized. We have not yet found that the views of experts on this question depend in any degree upon their politics or prejudices.

They depend only, so far as our researches have revealed, upon the extent of the particular expert's knowledge. We have found that the men who know most are the most gloomy.

Here, then, is the problem which we present to you, stark and dreadful and inescapable: Shall we put an end to the human race; or shall mankind renounce war? People will not face this alternative because it is so difficult to abolish war.

The abolition of war will demand distasteful limitations of national sovereignty. But what perhaps impedes understanding of the situation more than anything else is that the term "mankind" feels vague and abstract. People scarcely realize in imagination that the danger is to themselves and their children and their grandchildren, and not only to a dimly apprehended humanity. They can scarcely bring themselves to grasp that they, individually, and those whom they love are in imminent danger of perishing agonizingly. And so they hope that perhaps war may be allowed to continue provided modern weapons are prohibited.

This hope is illusory. Whatever agreements not to use H-bombs had been reached in time of peace, they would no longer be considered binding in time of war, and both sides would set to work to manufacture H-bombs as soon as war broke out, for, if one side manufactured the bombs and the other did not, the side that manufactured them would inevitably be victorious.

Although an agreement to renounce nuclear weapons as part of a general reduction of armaments would not afford an ultimate solution, it would serve certain important purposes. First, any agreement between East and West is to the good in so far as it tends to diminish tension. Second, the abolition of thermo-nuclear weapons, if each side believed that the other had carried it out sincerely, would lessen the fear of a sudden attack in the style of Pearl Harbour, which at present keeps both sides in a state of nervous apprehension. We should, therefore, welcome such an agreement though only as a first step.

Most of us are not neutral in feeling, but, as human beings, we have to remember that, if the issues between East and West are to be decided in any manner that can give any possible satisfaction to anybody, whether Communist or anti-Communist, whether Asian or European or American, whether White or Black, then these issues must not be decided by war. We should wish this to be understood, both in the East and in the West.

There lies before us, if we choose, continual progress in happiness, knowledge, and wisdom. Shall we, instead, choose death, because we cannot forget our quarrels? We appeal as human beings to human beings: Remember your humanity, and forget the rest. If you can do so, the way lies open to a new Paradise; if you cannot, there lies before you the risk of universal death.

Resolution:

We invite this Congress, and through it the scientists of the world and the general public, to subscribe to the following resolution:

"In view of the fact that in any future world war nuclear weapons will certainly be employed, and that such weapons threaten the continued existence of mankind, we urge the governments of the world to realize, and to acknowledge publicly, that their purpose cannot be furthered by a world war, and we urge them, consequently, to find peaceful means for the settlement of all matters of dispute between them."

Max Born	Linus Pauling
Percy W. Bridgman	Cecil F. Powell
Albert Einstein	Joseph Rotblat
Leopold Infeld	Bertrand Russell
Frederic Joliot-Curie	Hideki Yukawa
Herman J. Muller	

Appendix II
Commencement Address
at American University
By President John F. Kennedy
June 10, 1963

President Anderson, members of the faculty, board of trustees, distinguished guests, my old colleague, Senator Bob Byrd, who has earned his degree through many years of attending night law school, while I am earning mine in the next 30 minutes, distinguished guests, ladies and gentlemen:

It is with great pride that I participate in this ceremony of the American University, sponsored by the Methodist Church, founded by Bishop John Fletcher Hurst, and first opened by President Woodrow Wilson in 1914. This is a young and growing university, but it has already fulfilled Bishop Hurst's enlightened hope for the study of history and public affairs in a city devoted to the making of history and to the conduct of the public's business. By sponsoring this institution of higher learning for all who wish to learn, whatever their color or their creed, the Methodists of this area and the Nation deserve the Nation's thanks, and I commend all those who are today graduating.

Professor Woodrow Wilson once said that every man sent out from a university should be a man of his nation as well as a man of his time, and I am confident that the men and women who carry the honor of graduating from this institution will continue to give from their lives, from their talents, a high measure of public service and public support. "There are few earthly things more beautiful than a university," wrote John Masefield in his tribute to English universities – and his words are equally true today. He did not refer to towers or to campuses. He admired the splendid beauty of a university, because it was, he said, "a place where those who hate ignorance may strive to know, where those who perceive truth may strive to make others see."

I have, therefore, chosen this time and place to discuss a topic on which ignorance too often abounds and the truth too rarely perceived. And that is the most important topic on earth: peace. What kind of peace do I mean and what kind of a peace do we seek? Not a Pax Americana enforced on the world by American weapons of war. Not the peace of the grave or the security of the slave. I am talking about genuine peace, the kind of peace that makes life on earth worth living, and the kind that enables men and nations to grow, and to hope, and build a better life for their children – not merely peace for Americans but peace for all men and women, not merely peace in our time but peace in all time.

I speak of peace because of the new face of war. Total war makes no sense in an age where great powers can maintain large and relatively invulnerable nuclear forces and refuse to surrender without resort to those forces. It makes no sense in an age where a single nuclear weapon contains almost ten times the explosive force delivered by all the allied air forces in the Second World War. It makes no sense in an age when the deadly poisons produced by a nuclear exchange would be carried by wind and water and soil and seed to the far corners of the globe and to generations yet unborn.

Today the expenditure of billions of dollars every year on weapons acquired for the purpose of making sure we never need them is essential to the keeping of peace. But surely the acquisition of such idle stockpiles – which can only destroy and never create — is not the only, much less the most efficient, means of assuring peace. I speak of peace, therefore, as the necessary, rational end of rational men. I realize the pursuit of peace is not as dramatic as the pursuit of war, and frequently the words of the pursuers fall on deaf ears. But we have no more urgent task.

Some say that it is useless to speak of peace or world law or world disarmament, and that it will be useless until the leaders of the Soviet Union adopt a more enlightened attitude. I hope they do. I believe we can help them do it. But I also believe that we must reexamine our own attitudes, as individuals and as a Nation, for our attitude is as essential as theirs. And every graduate of this school, every thoughtful citizen who despairs of war and wishes to bring peace, should begin by looking inward, by examining his own attitude towards the possibilities of peace, towards the Soviet Union, towards the course of the cold war and towards freedom and peace here at home.

First examine our attitude towards peace itself. Too many of us think it is impossible. Too many think it is unreal. But that is a dangerous, defeatist belief. It leads to the conclusion that war is inevitable, that mankind is doomed, that we are gripped by forces we cannot control. We need not accept that view. Our problems are manmade; therefore, they can be solved by man. And man can be as big as he wants. No problem of human destiny is beyond human beings. Man's reason and spirit have often solved the seemingly unsolvable, and we believe they can do it again. I am not referring to the absolute, infinite concept of universal peace and good will of which some fantasies and fanatics dream. I do not deny the value of hopes and dreams but we merely invite discouragement and incredulity by making that our only and immediate goal.

Let us focus instead on a more practical, more attainable peace, based not on a sudden revolution in human nature but on a gradual evolution in human institutions — on a series of concrete actions and effective agreements which are in the interest of all concerned. There is no single, simple key to this peace; no grand or magic formula to be adopted by one or two powers. Genuine peace must be the product of many nations, the sum of many acts. It must be dynamic, not static, changing to meet the challenge of each new generation. For peace is a process – a way of solving problems.

With such a peace, there will still be quarrels and conflicting interests, as there are within families and nations. World peace, like community peace, does not require that each man love his neighbor, it requires only that they live together in mutual tolerance, submitting their disputes to a just and peaceful settlement. And history teaches us that enmities between nations, as between individuals, do not last forever. However fixed our likes and dislikes may seem, the tide of time and events will often bring surprising changes in the relations between nations and neighbors. So let us persevere. Peace need not be impracticable, and war need not be inevitable. By defining our goal more clearly, by making it seem more manageable and less remote, we can help all people to see it, to draw hope from it, and to move irresistibly towards it.

And second, let us reexamine our attitude towards the Soviet Union. It is discouraging to think that their leaders may actually believe what their propagandists write. It is discouraging to read a recent, authoritative Soviet text on military strategy and find, on page after page, wholly baseless and incredible claims, such as the allegation that American imperialist circles are preparing to unleash different types of war, that there is a very real threat of a preventive war being unleashed by American imperialists against the Soviet Union, and that the political aims – and I quote – "of the American imperialists are to enslave economically and politically the European and other capitalist countries and to achieve world domination by means of aggressive war."

Truly, as it was written long ago: "The wicked flee when no man pursueth."

Yet it is sad to read these Soviet statements, to realize the extent of the gulf between us. But it is also a warning, a warning to the American people not to fall into the same trap as the Soviets, not to see only a distorted and desperate view of the other side, not to see conflict as inevitable, accommodation as impossible, and communication as nothing more than an exchange of threats.

No government or social system is so evil that its people must be considered as lacking in virtue. As Americans, we find communism profoundly repugnant as a negation of personal freedom and dignity. But we can still hail the Russian people for their many achievements in science and space, in economic and industrial growth, in culture, in acts of courage.

Among the many traits the peoples of our two countries have in common, none is stronger than our mutual abhorrence of war. Almost unique among the major world powers, we have never been at war with each other. And no nation in the history of battle ever suffered more than the Soviet Union in the Second World War. At least 20 million lost their lives. Countless millions of homes and families were burned or sacked. A third of the nation's territory, including two thirds of its industrial base, was turned into a wasteland -- a loss equivalent to the destruction of this country east of Chicago.

Today, should total war ever break out again – no matter how – our two countries will be the primary target. It is an ironic but accurate fact that the two strongest powers are the two in the most danger of devastation. All we have built, all we have worked for, would be destroyed in the first 24 hours. And even in the cold war, which brings burdens and dangers to so many countries, including this Nation's closest allies, our two countries bear the heaviest burdens. For we are both devoting massive sums of money to weapons that could be better devoted to combat ignorance, poverty, and disease. We are both caught up in a vicious and dangerous cycle, with suspicion on one side breeding suspicion on the other, and new weapons begetting counter-weapons. In short, both the United States and its allies, and the Soviet Union and its allies, have a mutually deep interest in a just and genuine peace and in halting the arms race. Agreements to this end are in the interests of the Soviet Union as well as ours. And even the most hostile nations can be relied upon to accept and keep those treaty obligations, and only those treaty obligations, which are in their own interest.

So let us not be blind to our differences, but let us also direct attention to our common interests and the means by which those differences can be resolved. And if we cannot end now our differences, at least we can help make the world safe for diversity. For in the final analysis, our most basic common link is that we all inhabit this small planet. We all breathe the same air. We all cherish our children's futures. And we are all mortal.

Third, let us reexamine our attitude towards the cold war, remembering we're not engaged in a debate, seeking to pile up debating points. We are not here distributing blame or pointing the finger of judgment. We must deal with the world as it is, and not as it might have been had the history of the last 18 years been different. We must, therefore, persevere in the search for peace in the hope that constructive changes within the Communist bloc might bring within reach solutions which now seem beyond us. We must conduct our affairs in such a way that it becomes in the Communists' interest to agree on a genuine peace. And above all, while defending our own vital interests, nuclear powers must avert those confrontations which bring an adversary to a choice of either a humiliating retreat or a nuclear war. To adopt that kind of course in the nuclear age would be evidence only of the bankruptcy of our policy – or of a collective death-wish for the world.

To secure these ends, America's weapons are nonprovocative, carefully controlled, designed to deter, and capable of selective use. Our military forces are committed to peace and disciplined in self-restraint. Our diplomats are instructed to avoid unnecessary irritants and purely rhetorical hostility. For we can seek a relaxation of tensions without relaxing our guard. And, for our part, we do not need to use threats to prove we are resolute. We do not need to jam foreign broadcasts out of fear our faith will be eroded. We are unwilling to impose our system on any unwilling people, but we are willing and able to engage in peaceful competition with any people on earth.

Meanwhile, we seek to strengthen the United Nations, to help solve its financial problems, to make it a more effective instrument for peace, to develop it into a genuine world security system – a system capable of resolving disputes on the basis of law, of insuring the security of the large and the small, and of creating conditions under which arms can finally be abolished. At the same time we seek to keep peace inside the non-Communist world, where many nations, all of them our friends, are divided over issues which weaken Western unity, which invite Communist intervention, or which threaten to erupt into war. Our efforts in West New Guinea, in the Congo, in the Middle East, and the Indian subcontinent, have been persistent and patient despite criticism from both sides. We have also tried to set an example for others, by seeking to adjust small but significant differences with our own closest neighbors in Mexico and Canada.

Speaking of other nations, I wish to make one point clear. We are bound to many nations by alliances. Those alliances exist because our concern and theirs substantially overlap. Our commitment to defend Western Europe and West Berlin, for example, stands undiminished because of the identity of our vital interests. The United States will make no deal with the Soviet Union at the expense of other nations and other peoples, not merely because they are our partners, but also because their interests and ours converge. Our interests converge, however, not only in defending the frontiers of freedom, but in pursuing the paths of peace. It is our hope, and the purpose of allied policy, to convince the Soviet Union that she, too, should let each nation choose its own future, so long as that choice does not interfere with the choices of others. The Communist drive to impose their political and economic system on others is the primary cause of world tension today. For there can be no doubt that if all nations could refrain from interfering in the self-determination of others, the peace would be much more assured.

This will require a new effort to achieve world law, a new context for world discussions. It will require increased understanding between the Soviets and ourselves. And increased understanding will require increased contact and communication. One step in this direction is the proposed arrangement for a direct line between Moscow and Washington, to avoid on each side the dangerous delays, misunderstandings, and misreadings of others' actions which might occur at a time of crisis.

We have also been talking in Geneva about our first-step measures of arm[s] controls designed to limit the intensity of the arms race and reduce the risk of accidental war. Our primary long range interest in Geneva, however, is general and complete disarmament, designed to take place by stages, permitting parallel political developments to build the new institutions of peace which would take the place of arms. The pursuit of disarmament has been an effort of this Government since the 1920's. It has been urgently sought by the past three administrations. And however dim the prospects are today, we intend to continue this effort – to continue it in order that all countries, including our own, can better grasp what the problems and possibilities of disarmament are.

The only major area of these negotiations where the end is in sight, yet where a fresh start is badly needed, is in a treaty to outlaw nuclear tests. The conclusion of such a treaty, so near and yet so far, would check the spiraling arms race in one of its most dangerous areas. It would place the nuclear powers in a position to deal more effectively with one of the greatest hazards which man faces in 1963, the further spread of nuclear arms. It would increase our security; it would decrease the prospects of war. Surely this goal is sufficiently important to require our steady pursuit, yielding neither to the temptation to give up the whole effort nor the temptation to give up our insistence on vital and responsible safeguards.

I'm taking this opportunity, therefore, to announce two important decisions in this regard. First, Chairman Khrushchev, Prime Minister Macmillan, and I have agreed that high-level discussions will shortly begin in Moscow looking towards early agreement on a comprehensive test ban treaty. Our hope must be tempered – Our hopes must be tempered with the caution of history; but with our hopes go the hopes of all mankind. Second, to make clear our good faith and solemn convictions on this matter, I now declare that the United States does not propose to conduct nuclear tests in the atmosphere so long as other states do not do so. We will not -- We will not be the first to resume. Such a declaration is no substitute for a formal binding treaty, but I hope it will help us achieve one. Nor would such a treaty be a substitute for disarmament, but I hope it will help us achieve it.

Finally, my fellow Americans, let us examine our attitude towards peace and freedom here at home. The quality and spirit of our own society must justify and support our efforts abroad. We must show it in the dedication of our own lives – as many of you who are graduating today will have an opportunity to do, by serving without pay in the Peace Corps abroad or in the proposed National Service Corps here at home. But wherever we are, we must all, in our daily lives, live up to the age-old faith that peace and freedom walk together. In too many of our cities today, the peace is not secure because freedom is incomplete. It is the responsibility of the executive branch at all levels of government – local, State, and National – to provide and protect that freedom for all of our citizens by all means within our authority. It is the responsibility of the legislative branch at all levels, wherever the authority is not now adequate, to make it adequate. And it is the responsibility of all citizens in all sections of this country to respect the rights of others and respect the law of the land.

All this – All this is not unrelated to world peace. "When a man's way[s] please the Lord," the Scriptures tell us, "He maketh even his enemies to be at peace with him." And is not peace, in the last analysis, basically a matter of human rights: the right to live out our lives without fear of devastation; the right to breathe air as nature provided it; the right of future generations to a healthy existence?

While we proceed to safeguard our national interests, let us also safeguard human interests. And the elimination of war and arms is clearly in the interest of both. No treaty, however much it may be to the advantage of all, however tightly it may be worded, can provide absolute security against the risks of deception and evasion. But it can, if it is sufficiently effective in its enforcement, and it is sufficiently in the interests of its signers, offer far more security and far fewer risks than an unabated, uncontrolled, unpredictable arms race.

The United States, as the world knows, will never start a war. We do not want a war. We do not now expect a war. This generation of Americans has already had enough – more than enough – of war and hate and oppression.

We shall be prepared if others wish it. We shall be alert to try to stop it. But we shall also do our part to build a world of peace where the weak are safe and the strong are just. We are not helpless before that task or hopeless of its success. Confident and unafraid, we must labor on—not towards a strategy of annihilation but towards a strategy of peace.

Appendix III
Declaration on the Right
of Peoples to Peace*

The General Assembly,

Reaffirming that the principal aim of the United Nations is the maintenance of international peace and security,

Bearing in mind the fundamental principles of international law set forth in the Charter of the United Nations,

Expressing the will and the aspirations of all peoples to eradicate war from the life of mankind and, above all, to avert a worldwide nuclear catastrophe,

Convinced that life without war serves as the primary international prerequisite for the material well-being, development and progress of countries, and for the full implementation of the rights and fundamental human freedoms proclaimed by the United Nations,

Aware that in the nuclear age the establishment of a lasting peace on Earth represents the primary condition for the preservation of human civilization and the survival of mankind,

Recognizing that the maintenance of a peaceful life for peoples is the sacred duty of each State,

1. Solemnly proclaims that the peoples of our planet have a sacred right to peace;

2. Solemnly declares that the preservation of the right of peoples to peace and the promotion of its implementation constitute a fundamental obligation of each State;

3. Emphasizes that ensuring the exercise of the right of peoples to peace demands that the policies of States be directed towards the elimination of the threat of war, particularly nuclear war, the renunciation of the use of force in international relations and the settlement of international disputes by peaceful means on the basis of the Charter of the United Nations;

4. Appeals to all States and international organizations to do their utmost to assist in implementing the right of peoples to peace through the adoption of appropriate measures at both the national and the international level.

---

*G.A. res. 39/11, annex, 39 U.N. GAOR Supp. (No. 51) at 22, U.N. Doc. A/39/51 (1984).

ABOUT THE EDITOR

David Krieger is a founder of the Nuclear Age Peace
Foundation and has served as President of the Foundation since
1982. He has lectured throughout the United States, Europe
and Asia on issues of peace, security, international law, and the
abolition of nuclear weapons. He serves as an advisor to many
peace organizations around the world and has received many
awards for his work for a more peaceful and nuclear weapons-
free world. He is the author and editor of numerous books on
peace in the Nuclear Age. Among his books are *The Challenge
of Abolishing Nuclear Weapons; At the Nuclear Precipice: Catastrophe
or Transformation?; God's Tears: Reflections on the Atomic Bombs
Dropped on Hiroshima and Nagasaki* (Poetry); *The Doves Flew
High* (Poetry); *Hold Hope, Wage Peace; Einstein – Peace Now!;
Today Is Not a Good Day for War* (Poetry); *Peace 100 Ideas; Hope
in a Dark Time, Reflections on Humanity's Future; The Poetry of
Peace;* and *Choose Hope: Your Role in Waging Peace in the Nuclear
Age.* He is a graduate of Occidental College, and holds M.A.
and Ph.D. degrees in political science from the University of
Hawaii and a J.D. from the Santa Barbara College of Law.

INDEX

ABOUT THE FOUNDATION

The Nuclear Age Peace Foundation is a non-profit, non-partisan international organization. Since 1982, it has initiated and supported worldwide efforts to enhance both global and human security and is a voice for millions of people concerned about the fate of the planet. The Foundation has consultative status to the United Nations Economic and Social Council and is recognized by the UN as a Peace Messenger Organization.

VISION

Our vision is a just and peaceful world, free of nuclear weapons.

MISSION

To educate and advocate for peace and a world free of nuclear weapons, and to empower peace leaders.

HEADQUARTERS

PMB 121, 1187 Coast Village Road, Suite 1
Santa Barbara, CA 93108-2794
Telephone: (805) 965-3443
Fax: (805) 568-0466
E-mail: wagingpeace@napf.org

WEB PRESENCE

We invite you to learn more about the Foundation's programs by visiting our websites.
www.wagingpeace.org | *www.nuclearfiles.org*

Made in the USA
Lexington, KY
04 January 2012